Let the Ladybug Dance

Jacki London

Published By:
Jasher Press & Co.
www.jasherpress.com
customerservice@jasherpress.com
1.888.220.2068
New Bern, NC 28561

Copyright© 2014

ISBN: **978-0692211090**

First Edition
Printed and bound in the United States of America

LET THE Ladybug DANCE

JACKI LONDON

JASHER PRESS & CO.

Table of Contents

I dedicate "Let The Ladybug Dance" to my brother, Foster "Dickie" Barfield, Jr.

Dickie, I love you and I will always remember the ladybugs you would find for me and put in a jar for my birthday. To this day, I love ladybugs~

You promised me you would come to church with me the Sunday of my birthday, but unfortunately you went to be with the Lord that Thursday. Very sad, I went to church that Sunday without you. As I was leaving the church~ one of my dear members, Kim McCallop, said to me, "Pastor London, you have a bug in your hair." I replied, "Please get it out!" When she put it in my hand~ it was a ladybug! Tears begin to sneak out of my eyes because I knew that God had a way of letting me know that you did not forget to attend church with me.

Sleep well, Dickie~ I love you yesterday. I love you today. But not more than I will tomorrow.

Your sister,
Jacki

{ MEMORIES

LET THE LADYBUG DANCE....

Like a peeping Tom~
I watched you dance like a
ladybug
So free but yet so bound
You floated like a gift from
above
Controlling the room with
your wandering eyes
Enticing the air with your
breath
As though you were a
newborn baby
Your hair had grown so white
and soft
As though I remembered it
before
The hands of a warrior still moving gracefully
Thrilled by the moment~ the thief was watching
In and out, sweetly to and fro, my eyes glimpsed your body
Feeling every move within your soul
And the pounding of your chest
As a dagger piercing so deep to breathe once again
With tears from your eyes that never waxed dim
You looked at the Master and in a whisper, you spoke…
"let the ladybug dance forever and three days."

Jacki London
3/21/13

DANCE

Dance oh woman of brokenness
Dance oh woman of shame and guilt
Dance oh barren woman
Dance when you don't feel like dancing
Dance until you get tired of being shamed
Dance until you get tired of being guilty
Dance until you get tired of being barren
Dance into a new day
Dance into purity, holiness, and fruitfulness
Dance until you can't dance no more…

Jacki London
2013

GOOD MORNING

1 walk through the garden
as I walk
i know the aura is
of many things
the dew has already taken its form
the aroma of the roses has risen
making the birds chirp
even though you can't see them
you wonder if you should know
the lyrics to their song
yonder i see butterflies
ready to take flight
the brook is so cool
you think
how long will you flow
but wait
the sun
reflecting on my face
a brightness that caused
me to look up
to hear a small still voice say
good morning, I'm glad you're here

Jacki London
1995

13

.

Sometimes after retreating to my hotel room
from preaching an intensified revival~
"there" is when and where I realize I'm just
another human being ~
 (J. London)

SUMBODY STILL WATCHING O'ER ME

i can't find no res' on my steps
down 'en de basement
'da ain't no joy
i go out back
sumbody's always
messin'
wit' me
'da ain't no peace
i come in my sittin'
room
 ain't no love
i get weary- where has evert'ing gone
i go to my closet
ya' know da' secret one
the place where i can stretch forth my soul
and still be me
den i smile 'cause i'm glad to know
afterall, i ain't alone
sumbody still watching o'er me

Jacki London
1995

How Long, How Long

in the noon of the day
i go to a place on the other side of town

there's a glass window that causes me to stare
but for years there's never been anybody there

as tears grip my eyes and loneliness rip my heart
the emptiness i feel, ask

    "how long, how long?"

just as i turn to walk away
i feel the comfort and love of a strong voice
whisper...

    "not long, my dear – not long at all!"

Jacki London
1995

19

LOOK

i stumbled to fall
then looked to see who saw
i saw nothing but a strong wind
only to say…
look!
i paid for it all ~

Jacki London
1995

Don't loose your sense of possibility…
that's where your faith lies… in the end,
faith makes the impossible possible.
(J. London)

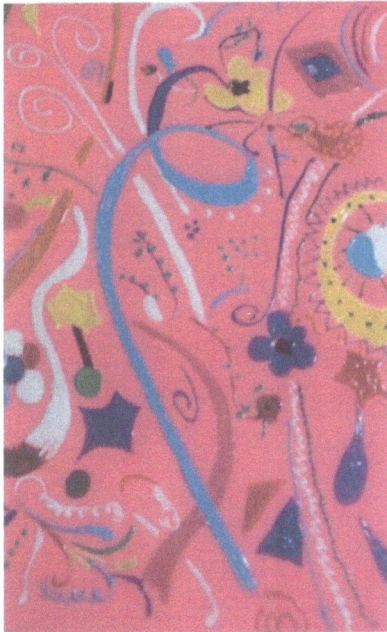

MY RED COWBOY HAT

As the dew settled on my new red suede cowboy boots
On my way to destiny
I made an unscheduled stop ~ in the valley
Had on my best… that is my red vest
Sparkling with gold studs on top
my brass buckled belt shined like
the sun
I put it on just for fun
Just a stone's throw away~
laid my red cowboy hat
On the rock I sat
Looking over clouds-
While waiting my turn-
I laughed out loud
When a soft voice said,
You'll be dead ~ if you don't learn
'good things come to those who wait'
But my mind was in a bad state
Made me be anxious
there I was
Thinking I was "such a much"
Just 'cause I was dressed up just a touch-
Couldn't hardly wait
To meet ole' man Death ~ had all kinds of enticing things
Smooth, cool, and walked with a swag
he was my date
Betta hurry, 'cause I dare not be late
So I grabbed my red cowboy hat
Flipped it on from where I sat
Suddenly, shaken by a thought…
Hold up! I can't be bought.
It ain't for me to leave

I believe
Just to go back where I've been
Ain't nothing there but a world of sin.
When I looked over at the clouds
I heard the wind so sharp
'til it pierced my soul as though it was a harp
A still voice rumbled while whispering so kind

"Hi, my name is destiny – I've been waiting on you for a long time."

Jacki London
9/09

Who we are is predetermined… unless you disregard that which has been predetermined

~

(J. London)

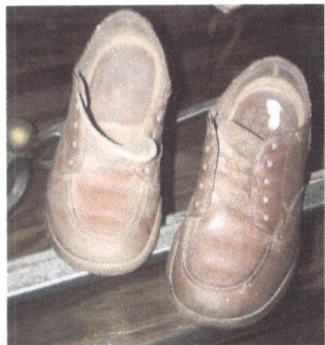

DID YOU MEAN TO HURT ME

Did you mean to hurt me
When you said good-bye
Did not you know
I would go down on my knees
And pray… "Jesus, please!"
Did you mean to hurt me
Knowing pain would leave me insane

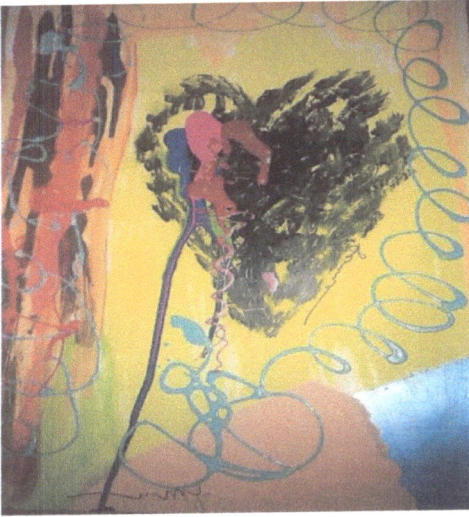

Or was that
your aim
Did you think I
would not be
strong
And break nor
last long
As you
whispered~
"Only the
strong survive-
the weak fall
by the way
side,"
Many nights I
cried~
"Thank you Lord for being my guide!"
Did you mean to hurt me
When you said yesterday had failed
My lips trembled ~ as I stated
"How could you forget and have no regret?"
Did you mean to hurt me
When you never said a word
Your footsteps were all I heard

My heart praised- "Thank you God,
Through it all ~ you did not let me fall!"
No, you did not hurt me ~ it was purpose
Because of you I learned ~ I have much to gain…
There is purpose in pain

Jacki London
2013

When you can't take no more… God won't
let you take no more
~ (J. London)

YOKED

it seemed as though
i remembered you from
the beginning of time
as my soul
  again
danced from the melodies
of your sweet nothin's
   i knew that it was you
when the moon shined
into your fiery eyes making
my heart ignite
into drops of blood
that dripped to your every command
  just as before
    i knew that it was you
when i felt the laughter
of your conniving voice
consume my body
only to chill my spirit
  i remembered
    i knew you from before
i glimpsed to search
 the secrets of your soul
  but
i became entangled
by the mystical aroma
of your breath
that whispered
    do you remember me
it was then
that I bit into your lips
to see if i'd remember
but the glare of vagueness

eluded my every thought

  i imagined to remember
but just as before
i was yoked
by the taste of cherries
that sweetly melted onto me
as though it was hot red lava
that seduced my mind
to the point of no return
           i knew that it was you
as i blinked my eyes
i looked at your feet
only to see footprints
pointing to the unknown
           then i remembered
just as before
i dreamed a dream
before its time

Jacki London
1995

GOOD TABOO

With the innocence of a sheep
You watch his swag
He awakens your cry to touch
The taboo feels good
But yet causes total silence
You loose your interest
~ so you think

But again you lied
Wondering who knows your thought
While your mind moves with his body
You become spaced
To another place in time
Shaking your head in shame
Your heart ask~
Why does simple pleasure hurt
Although your eyes bleed for more
They cry out in anguish
For just one touch
Time won't stand still
So you continue to watch
In silence
For fear
He might vanish

Jacki London
2013

STAY

the hour is late

almost midnight
why won't you *stay*
the need you desire
is just about here
please stay
don't get confused
your feelings or thoughts
are real
don't try to imagine
touch or see
just *stay*
wait but watch
so that you won't
miss the majesty of a
specialness that will
renew and ignite
therefore *stay*
never leave
if you shall
you just might miss
what you been
wanting to feel forever
time stands still
when you wait

but for reasons unknown
it's worth the wait
stand still and *stay*
the hour is ready
for you to know
that these things
only
come to those who *stay*

Jacki London
1995

When people don't know you, they fear you,
when they fear you, they find a reason to
dislike you ~
(J. London)

MR. MAN

you were there –
then you disappeared
into a vacuum –
leading to a realm so
mysterious
i try to walk with you
but i walk alone
i can't find you
i'm disturbed – i'm
lonely
emptiness is me
i can't feel you
i'm scared –
i need you
i look through a rose
pedal –
only to remember what
could have been
my heart has vanished
my mind is drifted
into that vacuum
only to realize
it never was.

Jacki London
1995

REMEMBERING...

I do not know
how I
remembered
to remember what
I remembered
All I know it was
good that I was
able to remember
What I did
remember

Because I thought I forgot to
remember
something very important to
remember
even when life does not want me
to remember
I will always remember
That my later days shall be
greater than my former days

Jacki London
10/22/13

Oftentimes the greatest conflicts come from within ~
(J. London)

AT NIGHT

The night is so
hot ~ nothing
but a plot
Shadows of
pain ~
I hate the night
Nothing to
gain
It ought to be a
shame
At night ~ so
many games
And you ask yourself
Why am I here
Seeking answers here and there
Captive by the moment
From fragrances of an evil scent
I hate the night
Nothing seems right
Everything's moving
Everything's grooving
Dancing to the wicked man's laugh
No rest for the weary ~ everything seems contrary
Born of trouble and for a few days
Still you continue in all the wrong ways
Sitting here in silence
Bound ~ waiting to be free
I hate the night ~ Wish I could take flight

Hoping maybe I'll vanish
And no one will see
That I was caught up
In the night so hot
Shaking my head
Cause It's nothing but a plot.

Jacki London
2010

How can a person be in the midst of great pain and have great joy at the same time unless there be a True and living God ~
(J. London)

I AM A SOLDIER WHO WON

My head is lifted firm
so are my shoulders, very stern
Like a soldier ~
Beatened but solid
Battered but bold…
Strong is my confidence
Joy is my strength
Through the storms of life
It was peace that carried me
But it was in the valley
I found my comfort zone.

My tears are memories
That remind me of where
I've been
But the laughter in my soul
Tells me destiny can no
longer wait
I know my purpose is greater
than where I've been
I am going where soldiers can only go
Then will I march in victory
To that upward journey
I will climb
To prove
I did not loose
I've already won

So many battles
Have caused me to be tested
Look at the battles scars
The story they tell seems sad
Don't feel sorry for me

51

Because they don't move me
I'm humbled to know
They only prove that I know where I've been
I know who I am
I am a winner who will never loose

I got on my war clothes, again, today
Proudly I wear them
with blood, sweat, and tears
Look at them… they are dirty
They are torn
They are worn
But they represent I won
I am a winner who could not loose
I am a soldier who did not die
Some soldiers don't win
But thank God, I am a soldier who won.

Jacki London
9/30/13

Let the Ladybug Dance

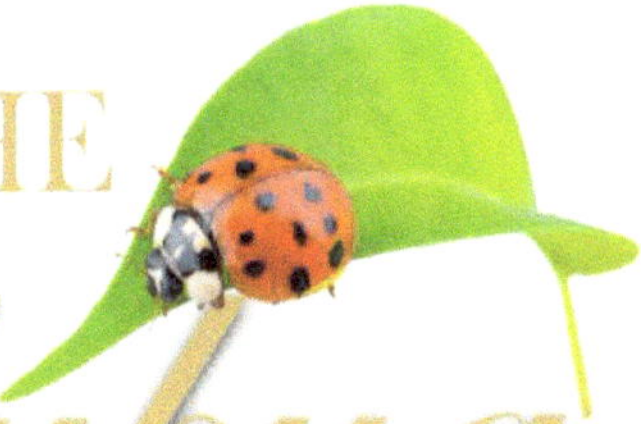

Jacki London

Jacki London born to SFC Foster and Lillian Barfield in Colorado Springs, Colorado. She became a Born again Believer in 1985 and licensed minister in 1987 through the Biblical House of God under the leadership of Dr. Alphonso Jackson. Later, God envisioned Prophetess London to establish an outreach ministry, Jacki London Ministries, which became incorporated through the State of North Carolina in 1991.

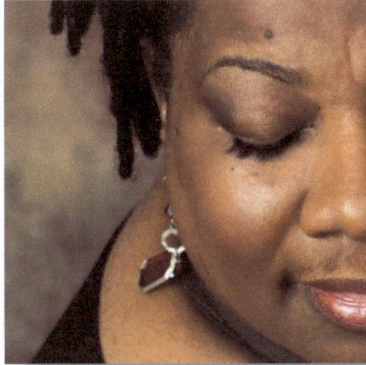

Jacki London is a national and international revivalist who is known and established in the office of the Five Fold Ministry. She has conducted several seminars and conferences. Just to name a few: "Can You Help A Sista Out" Retreat and Conference and Apostolic Prayer Conference. Also, she has birthed an annual event, the "War Brides In Red," a gala dinner after recognizing five outstanding women and three adolescent females in Southeastern North Carolina to benefit the Domestic Violent Shelter of Duplin County.

London is the host for the Apostolic Prayer Conference Line every Tuesday night that gather 100+ callers.

She has graduated 325 students from New Ministers Class which is a 10 week class held annually grooming and preparing young ministers to launch their ministries. The classes taught are: How to Prepare and Present A Sermon; Pulpit Etiquette, World Religions; Overview of Theology; Theological Vocabulary; Synoptic Gospels; Letters of Paul; Pre-Exilic and Post-Exilic Prophets; Pedo Baptism; The Eucharist; Weddings, Funerals, and many more subjects.

In 1998, POF Worship Center was birthed out of a 4-cord prayer meeting. This prayer meeting is at 8:00 every Monday nights the "house meetings" transitioned into something more massive – an establishment of worship that went from Monday evening services to Sunday morning traditional services with a membership of seven. God gave us favor in Pamlico County – some say "the back side of the mountain" – for five years; after which Pillar of Fire Worship Center relocated to Warsaw, NC where they currently hold services.

London is the Overseer of four Apostles, eleven Prophets, four Pastors and Teachers, five Evangelist/Elders, and two Spiritual Church Mothers.

Prophetess London holds an Associate's degree in Psychology from Craven Community College, A Bachelor of Science Degree in Religion from Mt. Olive College, a Master's Degree in Theology and a Doctorate in Theology through the North Carolina School of Theology.

She is in the preliminary stages of collecting data for several publishing's one being, "Super Tuesday On Mondays." Also, she is drawing plans for the envisioned gospel social club- "Solomon's Porch."

In her spare time, she is pampering her business "Lillian Bess" an interior design and gift shop. Her hobbies are listening to music, abstract painting, decorating, and entertaining.

Dr. London has 2 daughters; deShauna and Passion; six lovely grandchildren, who she says are the "apple of her eye": Lillian O'brien, deShon Montreal, Vinson Elijah, Shaakira Caleb, Kahlil, and Makalia Kodee.